Indy Cars

Jesse Young

Illustrated with photography from
the Indianapolis Motor Speedway

Reading consultant:

John Manning, Professor of Reading

University of Minnesota

Capstone Press

MINNEAPOLIS

Printed in the United States of America.

Capstone Press • 2440 Fernbrook Lane • Minneapolis, MN 55447

Editorial Director   John Coughlan
Managing Editor   John Martin
Copy Editor   Gil Chandler

Library of Congress Cataloging-in-Publication Data

Young, Jesse, 1941-
    Indy cars / by JesseYoung.
        p. cm. -- (Cruisin')
    Includes bibliographical references and index.
    ISBN 1-56065-222-5
    1. Automobiles, Racing--History--Juvenile literature.
  2. Indianapolis Speedway Race--Juvenile literature.
  [1. Indianapolis, Racing--History.   2. Automobile racing
  3. Indianapolis Speedway Race.]   I. Title. II. Series
  TL236.Y68   1995
  796.7'2--dc20   94-26766
                                                        CIP
                                                        AC

ISBN: 1-56065-222-5

99 98 97 96 95   8 7 6 5 4 3 2 1

Table of Contents

Chapter 1

The Roar of the Crowd

The fans at the Indianapolis 500 love cars. It is written all over their clothes, which display Ford, STP, Goodyear, Pennzoil, and other brands. As they stroll through the crowds, everyone talks about cars.

But a hush comes over the crowd when a voice booms, "Gentlemen, start your engines!"

The Roar of the Cars

The engines roar louder than jet airplanes on takeoff, and the cars speed by at over 200 miles (320 kilometers) per hour. Thousands of people watch and cheer. This is the Indianapolis 500.

Every year on Memorial Day weekend, the Indianapolis 500 takes place at the Indianapolis Motor Speedway. Only the 33 fastest cars qualify to race. During the race, cars hit speeds of 240 miles (386.5 kilometers) per hour on the **straights**. For two and a half hours, the drivers concentrate only on winning the race.

The fans collapse into their seats, excited and tired. The noise and the heat don't bother them, because they're watching the most exciting cars in auto racing.

Chapter 2

Carl Fisher: The Man Who Started it All

Carl Fisher loved **vehicles**. He also loved competition. As a young man, he raced bicycles. When automobiles came along in the early 1900s, he was one of the first in Indianapolis, Indiana, to buy one. He put his bicycle aside and raced his car at county fairs.

One day, on the way home from a business trip to Dayton, Ohio, Carl and a friend had car trouble. They managed to fix the problem.

Carl Fisher

Racers jockey for position at an early Indy race.

But it still bothered Carl that automobile makers were not improving their cars.

Carl Fisher's Idea

Carl Fisher had an idea. If he built a race track in Indianapolis, he could inspire American automobile manufacturers to make better cars. He believed automakers would try

to produce the best cars possible in order to win the race.

To interest the automakers, Fisher offered the winner $14,250. In 1911, the year of the first Indianapolis 500, that was a huge amount of money.

Chapter 3

Indy Cars from Start to Finish

Early Indy car builders used heavy sheet metal. The cars had spoked wheels and sat high off the ground. A huge engine sat under the hood in front and ran on gasoline. Today's Indy cars are much lighter and many times faster. Compared to the early cars, they look like spaceships.

Penske and Lola are the top race-car makers today. Their cars have won many Indianapolis 500 races. To buy one you would need to spend a lot of money.

Modern Indy cars hit 240 miles (360 kilometers) per hour on the straightaway.

An investment of $200,000 will buy only the **monocoque chassis**. This chassis includes the body, the frame, the wheels, and the **suspension**.

Made of **aluminum** and **carbon fiber**, the chassis is much lighter than the sheet metal chassis of early cars. **Fiberglass** covers the outside and gives modern Indy cars their shiny finish.

Designed For Speed

The nose of the Indy car is low to the ground and pointed. Inside, it has a hollow space for the driver's legs and feet. A quick-fill valve on the side of the car allows for fast refueling during pit stops.

Indy car builders have added wings to the cars to give them **downforce**. There is a **wing** attached to each side of the nose, and another one in the rear of the car. The wings on Indy cars have the opposite effect of an airplane's wings.

The aerodynamic shape of an Indy car helps it move smoothly on the track at top speed.

An aircraft's wings lift it into the sky. Indy car wings keep the fast-moving vehicle on the ground.

Indy cars also have **side pods** that contain radiators and other parts. A curved bottom is another special feature. When the car is moving, air passes under the side pods. The air enters the hollow of the curved bottom,

The wings in front and back help Indy cars stay on the ground at high speeds.

creating an area of low pressure. At the same time, higher pressure air on top of the car pushes down.

These **ground effects** give the Indy cars the downforce they need to stay firmly on the track at high speeds.

The Indy Car Engine

Indy teams spend about $100,000 for each engine. An engine lasts only one race before it needs to be rebuilt.

Engine makers such as Chevrolet, Cosworth, and Honda compete to make the fastest **V-8 engines** possible. Indy car engines put out 750 to 900 **horsepower**. The engines may be as large as 2.65 liters (162 cubic inches).

Rules allow the racing teams to **turbocharge** the engines. Turbocharging increases the air flow to the engine and gives better performance.

The **fuel cell** holds methanol instead of gasoline. Methanol keeps the engine cooler than gasoline. Indy cars burn about 1.5 gallons (5.7 liters) of methanol every 2.5 miles (4.1 kilometers).

Early Indy cars always used front-mounted engines. In 1961, Jack Brabham, an Australian, entered the Indianapolis 500 with a rear-engine car. Today, all Indy car engines sit behind the drivers.

Tires

Indy car tires are designed to give the cars maximum speed. The Goodyear company has spent years trying to make the best racing tires possible. Goodyear supplies all the tires for the Indianapolis 500. In return for tires, racing teams display the Goodyear name on their cars and driving equipment.

Computers

Computers inside Indy cars monitor speed, oil pressure, downforce, and engine performance. These computers send information to a **trackside** computer. The racing team watches this computer for clues to how the car is performing.

The monocoque chassis, the ground effects, the engine, the tires, and the computer are all designed to make an Indy car go faster.

Chapter 4

Safety: More than a Seatbelt

With Indy cars now topping 200 miles (322 kilometers) per hour, safety has become more important.

The lightweight chassis of an Indy car is made so the wheels will fall off in a crash. This lets the car slide instead of tumble. If the car does start to tumble, a **roll bar** behind the seat protects the **cockpit** and driver.

The cockpit, where the driver sits, is also made for safety. A seatbelt holds the driver in place, and padding behind the seat and on the steering wheel cushions the driver. Inside the nose of the car is a metal plate to protect the driver's feet.

In Case of Fire

Fires often start after a crash. Indy car drivers use special equipment for fire protection. The first line of defense is a fire extinguisher which discharges automatically during a fire.

Drivers wear a **balaclava** under their helmets. This is a hood made of **Nomex**, a fire-resistant cloth. Indy drivers also wear gloves, shoes, socks, and underwear made of Nomex.

In the 1970s, new rules for Indy cars limited the amount of fuel they could carry to 40 gallons (151 liters). Less fuel means less risk of spilling and fire.

Indy drivers wear special fire-resistant hoods called balaclavas.

Because of these safety features and smoother driving surfaces, it is safer to race today at speeds of over 200 miles (322 kilometers) per hour than it was in the old cars at 75 miles (120.8 kilometers) per hour.

Chapter 5
Indy Car Tracks

When Carl Fisher built the Indianapolis Speedway in 1909, it was made of crushed stone and tar. But these materials quickly broke up into potholes. When the old cars hit these potholes, drivers often lost control and crashed. Many drivers were injured and some died on the early Indy track.

The next year, Carl Fisher replaced the stone and tar with bricks. This is how the Indianapolis Speedway got its nickname, "The Brickyard." Today, the track is paved with asphalt. There are only a few bricks at the start-finish line.

A view from the air of the Indianapolis Motor Speedway.

The Indianapolis Motor Speedway is still a 2.5-mile (4.2-kilometer) oval. The four turns on the track are sharp and slightly angled, or **banked**. The banking helps the cars turn the sharp corners at high speeds.

Other Tracks and Other Races

Indy cars race at other events besides the Indianapolis 500. Indy teams move their race cars from track to track in big trailers. Championship Auto Racing Teams (CART),

the sponsor of the Indy race car season,
organizes races from March until October.

Because of the different tracks, Indy car
racing is more difficult than any other kind of
auto racing. Indy drivers must race at top
speeds on several different types of courses.
Each type has its own problems and challenges.

There are long ovals, such as the
Indianapolis Motor Speedway. Short ovals,
like the Pennsylvania International, are only
one mile (1.6 kilometers) around. The cars

**The cars have changed, but the goal is the same—to be
the first to cross the finish line after 500 miles (800
kilometers) at top speed.**

race around these tracks counterclockwise, always making left turns.

During the racing season, Indy cars also race on road courses which use public streets and highways. Each year in Denver, Colorado, a temporary road course is set up around Civic Center Park. With 16 turns, this course is a real test of skill. Road courses have both right and left turns.

During the racing season, Indy drivers earn points at each race, depending on their finishes. The winner of each race receives 20 points, while those who finish second or worse receive fewer. The driver in twelfth place earns only one point. At the end of the racing season, the driver with the most points is declared the world champion.

Chapter 6

Teamwork

Before 1938, Indy mechanics rode in the race cars with the drivers. The mechanic's job was to keep the car running and to tell the driver what the other cars on the track were doing. If the car broke down, the mechanic would fix the car on the spot.

Modern Indy car drivers have a team of people working with them. Each team member has a job. Mechanics and engineers work on the engine and on the ground effects. A fabricator builds and repairs body parts. The scorer keeps track of the car's speed during the race.

Someone else makes sure the computers are working.

During the race a general manager talks to the driver through a radio headset. At the same time, the manager keeps a close eye on the data the car's computer sends to the trackside computer.

The men and women on an Indy team work hard to keep all the systems in the car running smoothly.

Competition

When Carl Fisher started the Indianapolis 500 more than 80 years ago, he dreamed that it would become the greatest race in the world. While his dream has come true, he probably never imagined the shape and speed of modern Indy cars.

Indy car makers, engine makers, and tire makers continue to look for ways to make better cars. Every year the Indy cars seem to get a little better, a little faster, and a lot more exciting.

Glossary

aluminum–a lightweight metal

balaclava–the fire-resistant hood worn under the driver's helmet

banked–a raised track that allows cars to speed through sharp turns

carbon fiber–a strong and lightweight material made by superheating fiber

chassis–the structure to which the engine, wheels, seat, and body parts are attached

cockpit–a compartment that holds controls, gauges, and the driver

downforce–the force produced by air passing over and under a moving car that presses the car to the ground

fiberglass–a material made up of fiber-filled glass

fuel cell–a fire-safe container that holds methanol fuel

ground effects–the specially designed parts of the racing car that help produce downforce

horsepower–a measure of an engine's strength. One horsepower equals the strength to move 550 pounds one foot per second.

monocoque chassis–a special race-car chassis that is based on the design of an airplane's fuselage

Nomex–a fire-resistant fabric

roll bar–a protective cage which surrounds the driver in his seat

side pods–containers on each side of the car that hold radiators and other parts

straights–on oval tracks, the two longest lengths between the four curves

suspension–a system of springs, shocks, and links that makes riding smoother

trackside–also called *the pit*. A spot where mechanics and engineers monitor and work on the car during the race

turbocharge–an engine that burns exhaust gases for an extra burst of power

V-8 engine–an engine with eight pistons arranged like the letter "V," four pistons on each side

vehicle–a mechanical device used for transporting people or things

wings–structures on the nose and back of the car that produce downforce

To Learn More

Andretti, Michael and Robert Carver. *Michael Andretti at Indianapolis*. New York: Simon and Schuster, 1992.

Dregni, Michael. *The Indianapolis 500*. Minneapolis: Capstone Press, 1994.

Murphy, Jim. *The Indy 500*. New York: Clarion Books, 1983.

Sullivan, George. *Racing Indy Cars*. New York: Cobblehill Books, 1992.

Wilkinson, Sylvia. *Champ Cars*. Chicago: Childrens Press, 1982.

A museum at the Indianapolis Motor Speedway displays over 200 cars. Look for the car that won the first Indianapolis 500 in 1911. Visitors can even buy a ticket to be taken for a ride around the race track.

Acknowledgments

Capstone Press wishes to thank the Indianapolis Motor Speedway for photo assistance and information; and Dan Cunningham & Mike Wara for help with technical information.

Index